I0148902

DANIEL
AND GOD'S SOVEREIGNTY

WHAT IT MEANS TO SAY GOD IS IN CONTROL

TERRELL CARTER

Energion Publications
Gonzalez, FL
2021

Copyright © 2023, Terrell Carter. All Rights Reserved.

Scripture quotations marked CEV are taken from the Contemporary English Version, Copyright © 1995 American Bible Society.

ISBN13: 978-1-63199-783-9
eISBN13: 978-1-63199-784-6

Energion Publications
P. O. Box 841
Gonzalez, FL 32560

pubs@energion.com
energion.com

DEDICATION

To the pastors, professors, and teachers who have helped to shape my understanding of God's love and sovereignty.

To the congregations that have been patient with me as I have attempted to preach and teach about God's love and sovereignty.

To Genevieve and Jerry Carter for embodying God's love and sovereignty for me and Derrell and for life more abundantly.

TABLE OF CONTENTS

PRELUDE

2020 (the time of this writing) has turned out to be anything but typical. A worldwide pandemic has emerged and brought with it an unimaginable loss of life and livelihood for so many people. The consistent questions the world asks when times are hard are "Where is God during the bad times? If God is so good and loving, why would God allow such widespread suffering? Why have so many people been allowed to die and so many lives changed in such negative ways? If God is so powerful, when will He show up and stop the pain?"

This is not the first time these types of questions have been asked. These types of questions have been asked throughout history. They served as part of the backdrop for one of the most famous books in the Bible. The Old Testament book of Daniel. You can hear these questions being asked in chapters 1-6 of Daniel as the writer of Daniel explores what it means for believers in God to try to remain in relationship with God when it seems like God is not present during their times of suffering. Daniel records the experiences of people whose faith was being stretched in ways that none of them could have previously imagined.

There is much that we can learn from them and what God, and the author of Daniel, was saying about God's presence and power during times of personal and national disruption. My hope in writing this book, which began as a series of sermons I delivered to the congregation where I serve as pastor, is to remind all of us that God is still present and involved, even when it does not seem like God is. Even during the times when we think God is absent, God is still bigger and more powerful than any personal hardship, national pandemic, or the silence we experience when times are hard. I pray that our faith in God, and in others, will be renewed and strengthened by the words found in this book.

Terrell Carter, DMin
Summer 2020

A Brief Note on the Authorship and Dating of Daniel

Multiple debates have occurred within the realm of Christian scholarship as to who authored the Book of Daniel and when it was composed. Some theologians believe the book was written by Daniel during his lifetime. Others contend that the book was composed generations later by several editors who wanted to use stories about Daniel that had been handed down over generations as a symbol of hope for people who were themselves experiencing pain and turmoil. There are other theories that fit between these two poles.

This book is not concerned with litigating the apologetic or theological arguments related to the potential author(s) or date(s) of writing of the Book of Daniel. My intent in writing this book was to examine the stories told in Daniel 1-6, understand what those stories would have meant to a reader living in and through an ancient Hebrew context, and, ultimately, explore and understand what the Book of Daniel could mean for contemporary readers in the 21st Century who experience life-altering and faith challenging circumstances.

GOD IS SOVEREIGN — AN INTRODUCTION TO DANIEL

DANIEL 1:1-2

I imagine that most of us are familiar with the book of Daniel. Some of the most famous and familiar stories that are found in the Bible come from Daniel. The story of Daniel in the lion's den, the three Hebrew boys, although they were probably men, in the fiery furnace, and a strange statue made of various metals, clay, and dirt that gets destroyed by a huge rock are likely the ones that are most familiar to us. Within the following pages, we will explore the book of Daniel to see what these, and other stories, can tell us about God and God's relationship to people.

We will explore the overarching theme of the book and try to understand how that theme can be applied to our lives on a regular basis. I'll just cut to the chase now and share what I understand the theme of Daniel to be. The overarching theme is that God is sovereign despite what things may look like. Although God is sovereign, God sometimes allows things to occur that we do not understand, and life may not go the way we envisioned, but even amid those realities, God is still in control. Due to the season of life they found themselves in, this theme was of the utmost importance to the people we encounter in Daniel, as well as for the audience that the book was written to. As you can imagine, I believe the theme of God's sovereignty is important for us, as well.

The author of Daniel shared the theme of God's sovereignty through two literary genres that are found in the book. Those genres are historic narratives, which are found in chapters 1-6, and apocalyptic writings which are found in chap-

1

ters 7-12. This book will only explore chapters 1-6. The first half of Daniel is narrative. Chapters 1-6 tell the story of what life was like for four men who belonged to the tribe of Judah and how life changed for them after their city was overtaken by a stronger foreign power. Although this is an experience that most of us will never experience, how Daniel and his friends responded to change in their lives can serve as an example for us to follow.

The narrative portion of Daniel's story asks multiple questions that are still relevant today: Was (is) God all-powerful? If God was (is) all-powerful, where was God when their city and nation were being defeated? How were they to live as captives in a strange city? Did God hold any expectations for them even though they were captives in a foreign land? How Daniel and his friends answered those questions would show the depth, or lack thereof, of their faith in God's sovereignty.

The second genre used in Daniel was apocalyptic writing. Apocalyptic means revealing or unveiling something that was hidden. Apocalyptic writing is a genre type that contains many different styles including, but not limited to, writings about future events. This example is going to sound goofy but think of a gameshow stage and in the middle of that stage is a covered table. Suddenly the game show host pulls the cover off the table revealing keys to a new car. That's what apocalypse means. The act of making something visible, or understandable, that previously was hidden. But, instead of revealing gifts on game shows, it involves revealing spiritual and theological truths.

In general, the spiritual and theological truths that are most often associated with apocalyptic literature in the Bible are the themes of Daniel: Because God is sovereign, God's children could stand strong in whatever tribulations they were experiencing because God would eventually save them. And, with God's salvation would come a new order for life.

As we begin to explore Daniel, I want to acknowledge that we can sometimes experience challenges reading the book. There are two brief reasons I think this is possible. First, the language and imagery employed by the writer of Daniel, especially in chapters 7-12, are not always familiar to us. As we shall see, there are titles used in Daniel, like the Son of Man (which will not be explored in this book), that are unfamiliar to our context. This unfamiliarity can cause us to misunderstand some of the main points the writer intended to make.

Second, we can experience problems in reading Daniel because we often think that the book is primarily about prophecy and end times information. Although those two things occur in the book, they are not the main themes or goals of the book. The main goal of Daniel is not to tell us about end-time events. Instead, it is to remind readers that God is sovereign over seen and unseen powers, and because of God's sovereignty, God's children never have to lose hope.

It's important for me to point out these two challenges of interacting with the two genres found in Daniel because as we explore the stories that occur within the pages of Daniel, we should understand that the genre that is being used in each chapter will affect how we read the verses and what we can anticipate learning and understanding about what the author is trying to tell us. Overall, Daniel tells a consistent and repetitive story of God's desires and intentions for God's interactions with humankind. Within the various stories found in the book, we will experience some of the same imagery and situations that are found in other portions of the Hebrew Bible.

For example, like Joseph in Genesis, Daniel and his friends were taken from their homeland and sent to a foreign kingdom. Like Joseph, dreams and the interpretation of dreams led to good and bad things occurring in the lives of the book's main characters. Like Joseph, the main characters exhibited great self-control and self-discipline, prayed regularly, and maintained personal integrity related to what God wanted for their lives. But this faithfulness led to people lying on them and them being unjustly punished. Living for God came at a price.

As found in other Old Testament passages, Daniel also shows us that his God, the invisible God, is more powerful than any visible kings or their invisible gods. Daniel's God is involved in the personal affairs of his followers. As seen in other Old Testament passages, what you see is not always how things are. Sometimes God's plans to act on behalf of God's people may be delayed due to people's sin or because of spiritual battles that occur behind the scenes. But no matter when God shows up, it is always on time.

For all the things I just said, I must admit that Daniel 1 begins in a way that is less than confidence-building for Daniel and his fellow citizens. Daniel 1 begins by acknowledging that the nation of Judah had been overcome by King Nebuchadnezzar and the powers of Babylon. King Nebuchadnezzar occupied the throne of the most powerful kingdom of the time. Babylon was a military threat to every nation in the region. Judah was one of the smallest nations in the region. So small that Judah, realizing that it could not stand up to Babylon's might by itself, agreed to partner with Egypt to push back against Babylon's steadily increasing footprint in the region.

This partnership between Judah and Egypt was a disastrous short-lived failure that ended with King Nebuchadnezzar and his army overrunning the city of Jerusalem, plundering the temple, the king of Judah and multiple other people from the community being taken to Babylon in chains, and the land left scarred. In addition to human bodies being taken to Babylon, artifacts from the temple in Jerusalem were taken and placed in the temple of Marduk, Babylon's primary god. This was nothing short of an embarrassment for Judah because outside of Ba'al, Marduk was the biggest competitor to the Hebrew God. This left God's children with a serious question to ponder. What did it mean for the armies of Marduk to overpower the armies of Judah?

In the thinking of the time, when a king won a battle against another nation, it was believed that he won because his god was bigger, stronger, and more powerful than the other king's god. Each nation believed that one of the reasons for following a god was because of that God's ability to bring its followers victory during war. Kings and nations took this idea so seriously that sometimes wars were conducted primarily to expand the territory and influence of a specific god.

At first glance, the actions recorded within Daniel 1:1-2 are a disaster. The city had been breached, the land destroyed, and the god of the Hebrews had been summarily overpowered, defeated, and proven to be less than a powerful god who was worth following. On the surface, or only through a quick reading, it looked like Nebuchadnezzar and his god were winners, and Judah and his God were losers. But, is that really the case?

The writer of Daniel leaves multiple clues throughout these two verses that show that is not what's really going on. The writer tells us that Nebuchadnezzar's victory was possible only because God allowed it. Different translations say it in different ways. One says that God gave the victory to Nebuchadnezzar. Another says God let him have victory over Judah. Another says that God handed him the victory. The point the writer was making was that Nebuchadnezzar's victory came not because of his military might but because God allowed it to occur as part of a larger plan God had going. Based on all that we know about Judah's relationship to God, we know what that plan was. Due to Judah's ongoing sin, God decreed that God would allow them to be overtaken by a stronger nation. Nebuchadnezzar just so happened to be the king of that nation.

This will not be the last time that the writer of Daniel clarifies the limits of Nebuchadnezzar's power over and against God and God's children. We will see in future chapters that Nebuchadnezzar became drunk with power after his victories and accomplishments and God reminded him that he was a mere human who also lived in subjection to God's power and will. Nebuchadnezzar should never forget that even when God allowed something to happen in Nebuchadnezzar's favor, God was actively allowing it to happen.

If what I believe is true and the overarching theme of Daniel is God's sovereignty, I can understand why an initial reading of Daniel 1:1-2 would leave people with multiple unanswered questions about God and God's trustworthiness. Why does God sometimes allow evil to prevail? Why does God not always show God's strength immediately? Although this is counter intuitive to us, it clearly is the mode by which God has chosen to operate.

Of this truth, Dr. Wendy Widder writes,

> The wisdom behind such apparent displays of weakness (by God) is not intuitive to us. We think God should always 'show up,' defeating his enemies and rescuing his people. In our way of thinking, he gets the most glory when everyone sees how powerful he is. Yet God regularly chooses to operate within the limitations of his creation rather than wowing the world with supernatural acts.[1]

What Daniel and friends, King Nebuchadnezzar, and anyone who was paying attention learned through the events recorded in Daniel was that God was sovereign and greater than any other god, king, or nation. Because of this, God's followers could stand strong in the face of uncertainty. When they did stand strong, God was pleased with them. God's enemies were to recognize God's authority and standing as the supreme God who was greater than any opposition. If God's enemies did not understand that, God would hold them accountable and punish them.

Daniel is ultimately a story of hope. Hope because God was (is) on the throne ruling over the world and humankind. Because God is in control, God's followers will not only survive hard times, but they can also thrive for God's glory.

---

1 Widder. *Daniel.* Zondervan, 2016. 15.

TAKING A STAND WITHIN GOD'S SOVEREIGNTY

DANIEL 1:3-16

I believe the overarching theme of the book of Daniel is that God is sovereign. No matter what things may look like, or who looks like they are in control, or how out of whack life may be, God is still all-powerful, and God occupies the throne of authority over all creation, always. The challenge we face in understanding God's sovereignty is that God may allow certain things to happen that we do not understand, or God may cause certain things to occur that we do not understand, or God may even use certain people in ways and for reasons we do not fully understand to accomplish God's goals. These are the realities of how the world operates within the parameters of God's sovereignty.

When we are faced with the realities of God's sovereignty and the mysteries that sometimes accompany that sovereignty, we are usually left with more questions than answers. One of the questions we usually must reckon with is that amid the fact that God sometimes causes and sometimes allows certain things to happen in the world that we do not understand, how do we remain faithful to what God is trying to do or bring about in our lives? Do we push back against the things that God causes or allows to happen in life, or do we accept them and try to understand what God wants to bring about within us as a result of those circumstances?

Do we seek to exhibit or attempt to retake a certain level of control over our lives when uncertainty occurs, or do we try to learn a way to live into what God is doing and trust that, even in discomfort, God will eventually show God's strength? This is the challenge that Daniel and his friends faced in Daniel 1:3-16. Life had

7

been turned upside down for them, yet, it was technically not as bad as it could have been.

They had lost control over their own lives in a most dramatic way, but they were better off than most of their countrymen. They had been taken away from their homeland, but they were about to be offered a special opportunity of service by the king. They would be servants of the king, but they would also be elevated to a position of prestige above everyone else from their homeland. With this new opportunity to serve the king and experience preferential treatment came a challenge. Would they fully buy into the gifts and opportunities the king was offering them, or would they stand strong in their heritage and faith and say no to the temptations that accompanied what the king was offering?

So, what was the king offering? He was offering them the opportunity to participate in a three-year-long process to learn about, and participate in, Babylonian culture. They would receive the best Babylonian food, learn about the religion Babylonians followed, and be educated about Babylonian culture. After that three-year process was complete, Daniel and his friends would be added to King Nebuchadnezzar's royal court as advisors, essentially serving as representatives for the king before their kinsmen.

The purpose of this training was to cause Daniel and his friends to assimilate Babylonian culture, to buy into it fully and to accept it as their own, and then go back to their people and tell them how wonderful life under Babylonian rulership was. King Nebuchadnezzar did not necessarily want these Hebrew youth to forget about their people or their homeland. Instead, he wanted them to become cheerleaders for why life for them and their countrymen would be better under his rulership and the rulership of his god Marduk.

The training offered by the king likely involved Daniel and his friends learning all there was to learn about the religion of Babylonia and how Babylonians believed Marduk was the most powerful god because he had given the king and his army victory over Daniel's people. The training also likely included Daniel and his friends learning practices related to divination. They would learn how to read signs and understand omens and other acts they believed originated from the spirit world. The goal of learning these things was to help them communicate with the gods of Babylon and understand how actions that occurred in this world fit into the plans of these other gods.

Do you see a problem with Daniel and his friends learning the art of divination? It was specifically forbidden by God. In multiple places in the Hebrew Bible, God said do not practice these kinds of things. In Deuteronomy 18:9-12 God said,

> When you come into the land that the Lord your God is giving you, you shall not learn to follow the abominable practices of those nations. There shall not be found among you anyone who burns his son or his daughter as an offering, anyone who practices divination or tells fortunes or interprets omens, or a sorcerer or a charmer or a medium or a necromancer or one who inquires of the dead, for whoever does these things is an abomination to the Lord. And because of these abominations the Lord your God is driving them out before you.[2]

The irony was that years after this command had been given by God, God allowed multiple people from Judah to be placed into a situation where they were being forced to practice the very things that God said were an abomination. As a side not, this will be the first of a few times where this type of irony comes up in the book of Daniel. We will see it again in Daniel 2.

I feel for Daniel and his friends because they did not have a choice in the circumstance. Well, they did have one choice. They could refuse to learn those things and refuse to participate in the process of assimilation, but they would end up losing their lives. It was much more expedient, and life-saving for them, to play the game and learn what the king wanted them to. Living in this world would not be easy. Their training not only involved new religious knowledge and practices, it involved new diets and new names.

---

2 Quoted from the Contemporary English Version.

The king understood that to truly cause his subjects to buy into their new roles, he had to change everything about their lives. This included what they ate and how they referred to themselves or how they thought about themselves.

Changing their diets was not an insignificant act. Food and access to it was a sign of stability, a sign of status, and even a sign that a certain god had smiled upon a person or people by providing them with the resources to feed themselves. Food was also a sign of power. If you controlled people's access to food, you would likely be able to obtain whatever you wanted from them. How they related to food was important for Daniel's identity and that of his friends. Their God had clearly outlined what they should and should not eat and how foods were to be prepared. God had also outlined that they could not eat any food that had been offered to other gods. The food available to Daniel and friends would violate most of these prohibitions. As we will see in a moment, Daniel did not go for this.

Changing their names was not an insignificant act, either. As we have talked about before, names also represented identity in Hebrew culture. When you were given a name, it represented your parent's hopes for you, or your name was an acknowledgment of God's past or future actions. It was rare for someone to change their name because it meant that expectations for that person were changing. King Nebuchadnezzar understood the power of changing someone's name. Dr. John Walton writes, "To change someone's name is to exercise authority over them and their destiny."[3] In changing their names, the king was planning to change the destiny and focus of Daniel and his friends.

As I think through all that Daniel and his friends experienced, this is where I find a dichotomy or variance. As we read their story, Daniel and his friends do not push back against the king on every change he makes in their lives. They do not push back against hav-

---

3 Walton, Matthews, and Chavalas. *The IVP Bible Background Commentary.* InterVarsity Press, 2000. 731.

ing their names changed. Instead, it seems that they accept them. Yet, they do push back against changes to their diet and foods they consume. Well, at least Daniel does. But even that is not a full push back or refusal.

Daniel 1:3-16 tells us that Daniel decided not to defile himself by eating and drinking what the king made available to them and instead to only eat the things that would not cause him to defile himself. In this instance, the word defile meant to make something or someone ethically or ritually unclean. To be ritually unclean meant that a person or thing was not fit to be presented to God or used in service for God due to a defect, an impurity, or something wrong with it. Since God was holy, anything that was going to enter God's presence or be used in service to God had to be clean, whole, complete, without defect, and the way God intended it.

What we do not usually understand is that a person or thing could be ritually unclean without it being sinful. Ritual cleanness was not primarily about sin. It had everything to do with something existing as God had intended it. An example would be when a baby eats breakfast and before it is all said and done, that child is a mess. You are preparing to go to work and you have on a new white suit or dress. Would you let that child run up to you and hug you? Probably not.

You would want that child to wash their hands and face first. You would not be mad at them, but you would not want your clothes to look like theirs. You would still love them. You would want them to be clean before you hugged them. That's ritual cleanness. It would make sense for Daniel to think that eating the king's food, which would have likely been offered to the god Marduk or in service to Marduk before it was made available to people in the king's court, would defile him. Again, God had spoken multiple times before about not eating food offered to other gods or idols.

The problem with thinking that Daniel took his stand against eating some of the king's food only because the food had likely been offered to Marduk is that even the vegetables that Daniel accepted and ate had likely been offered to Marduk too. It was likely that everything that Daniel and friends were offered had first been offered to Marduk. So, not eating any of the meat is meaningless because anything they ate, including the vegetables, was ritually contaminated, as well. And, God never stopped them from drinking wine in the first place.

But there is a second option that may better explain what Daniel may have been thinking. As I said, defilement included ritual uncleanness and ethical uncleanness. Ethical uncleanness involved making decisions to live in a way that was in opposition to the relationship God wanted to have with a person. It was intentionally living in such a way that a person could not enter God's presence, or be used by God, or participate in service to God because they were intentionally not living in ways that God wanted.

I imagine Daniel thought that willingly giving in to all the king's desires was akin to ethical uncleanness. No, Daniel and his friends could not push back against or resist every assimilation tactic the king instituted, but they could be strategic in how they continued to remember their God, even if it was through simple acts of protest. This act of resistance (remembrance) comes across not as a rally cry for an entire nation, but as a small personal victory for Daniel and his friends. That's okay. It was not necessary for everything they did to impact the entire nation. Ethical cleanness primarily involved personal actions and attitudes when life is difficult.

Of this idea, Dr. Wendy Widder writes, "Maybe the purpose of Daniel's resolution was less about making a public stand—as it is often portrayed—than making a private decision to remember the real source of life during the three years of total immersion training."[4] Although our lives are not as dire as Daniel and his friends, like them, we too still daily face the temptation to assimilate to a culture that, many times, stands in opposition to how God calls each of us to live. No, we have not been taken from our homes

4 Widder. *Daniel*. Zondervan, 2016. 30.

and forced to take no new names or any of the things that Daniel experienced.

Our assimilation is not forced upon us. Instead, it is offered to us, wrapped in packages that help put us at ease when we open them. Packages of comfort and stability, of progress and technology that will make our lives better, of financial security, and of fulfilling the American dream. Our assimilation is offered to us as the latest update or app on our phones and computers. Sometimes we accept these packages for the sake of the calling God has placed in all our lives. The calling to stand within God's sovereignty and to remember that none of these external things brings our lives meaning. Only our relationship with God fulfills that burning inner desire to have meaning.

I end this chapter with a simple quote from Dr. Daniel L. Smith-Christopher that I believe brings the point home. Dr. Smith-Christopher writes, "The message of Daniel 1 is a powerful reminder for us to search within ourselves for those aspects of 'the king's food and wine' that we ought to resist for the sake of the gospel message."[5] Which gifts from the king of this world do we all need to resist for God's glory? Only you can answer that question for yourself. Amen.

---

5 Smith-Christopher. *The New Interpreter's Bible Volume VII: Introduction to Apocalyptic Literature, Daniel, and the Minor Prophets.* Abingdon Press, 1997. 44.

NAVIGATING UNANTICIPATED RELATIONSHIPS WITHIN GOD'S SOVEREIGNTY

DANIEL 1:17-21

As much as we may wish it was not true, the world, and by default, our lives, are filled with interactions with people who do not always think like us, feel like us, or believe like us on any given subject. Have any of you experienced the reality of this truth recently? We work closely with, regularly interact with, and are even married to and related to people who think and act completely differently from us. And these people are not ashamed of the fact that they think and act differently than us. Many times, it seems like they are proud of their different ways of thinking and different ways of living and they look at us like we are the strange ones.

The reality of life is that we are all in relationship with someone or some people who live on the opposite side of life than us. Whether it is politically, socially, economically, spiritually, religiously, or whatever. When we interact with people like this, we may view them as an enemy and that they are just trying to be difficult people to make our lives hard, but that may not be the case. They may occupy a space or position opposite us by choice or by default or due to a series of unique life experiences that shaped and formed them in the past. And just because they occupy a space or position that is opposite us, does not necessarily make them bad people.

In God's sovereignty, God has created a world full of diverse people with diverse experiences. In God's sovereignty, we meet and interact with people who may be the opposites of us. In God's sovereignty, we do not get to only operate in a world filled with people who think, and act like us. This is an-

other difficult reality of God's sovereignty. These relationships with people who are different from us are not always bad things to experience. They may seem like an inconvenience for us, but sometimes these relationships serve a greater purpose for us and others. Ultimately, they serve the greater purpose of God's will being done in the world.

This is what I think is the point of Daniel 1:17-21, the conclusion of the first movement of the book of Daniel. Daniel 1 began with King Nebuchadnezzar overtaking Jerusalem and ends with four young men from Jerusalem becoming important officials within the king's royal court. Before we look at what these elevations to royal positions mean, I want to look at the literary technique which the writer of Daniel is using in these verses and will be used in some form all the way up to Daniel 6.

Have any of you who have read through the book of Daniel before recognized any similarities between the story of Daniel and other stories within the Hebrew Bible (Old Testament)? There is one storyline in Genesis that holds multiple similarities to Daniel. It's the story arc of Joseph, the boy with the technicolor coat. Okay, technically he does not have a technicolor coat, it is a coat of many colors, but I think you get the point. In Genesis, Joseph is intentionally described as handsome, which sometimes gets him into unintentional trouble. He's very faithful to God, which also gets him into trouble. He can interpret dreams. He understands that God has a bigger purpose for his life. Through his faithfulness to be a good servant of others, he is blessed and promoted, and others associated with him are blessed.

That sounds a lot like Daniel and his friends, does it not? Daniel and his friends were described as handsome and fit, although their good looks never got them into trouble. They were all faithful to God, which did get them into trouble. Daniel interpreted dreams and had dreams, himself, that angels had to interpret. Through their willingness to be faithful servants, even to a king

16

and kingdom that was not their own, they and others around them were blessed.

Biblical scholars classify these similar types of stories as court stories or courtier stories.

Court or courtier stories told the events surrounding how God used wise and pious individuals who, although they were imprisoned in a foreign land, somehow ended up overcoming unimaginable odds to succeed within the royal court of a foreign king. Courtier stories usually followed one of two plotlines. The first plotline was the occurrence of a conflict in the royal court which stemmed from the hero(ine) of the story, for example, Joseph or Daniel, sticking to his moral compass or his faith in God. That faithfulness put the hero(ine) into danger, and it took an act of God to get them out of danger.

The second typical court story involved a contest in a royal court setting where the hero(ine) and sometimes the rest of the court officials faced a challenging problem that had them stumped. Eventually, the hero(ine) is the only person that is wise enough to figure out how to overcome the challenge or strong enough to overcome it. After exhibiting such a greater level of wisdom than everyone else in the court, the person is rewarded with a new position or the fulfillment of a request or need that blesses more than just the wise hero.

Before anyone thinks that I'm saying the Bible is only a story or the events in Daniel are only stories, that is not what I'm saying. I believe the Bible and believe in the history of the Hebrew people. What I'm trying to point out right now is that it seems like the writers of the Hebrew Bible used similar techniques over multiple generations and genres to tell stories about their history and their understanding of God's faithfulness and sovereignty. These stories are the foundation of the Bible and these practices of using similar literary techniques throughout the Old Testament to share and explain their history are some of the things that help make the Bible a unified story that clearly tells the story of God's love for this people and all creation.

I also think these common techniques served a greater purpose as well. I think these similar stories or similar ways of retelling the history of the Hebrew people served to remind readers of God's sovereignty from generation to generation and to encourage future generations to trust in God's sovereignty and to embrace as their own the hope of past generations. Dr. Widder writes, "The court stories…reminded beleaguered Jews that even though foreign kings raged around them, the God of Israel was still on the throne. Human power was only derived, given, and taken away by the sovereign Most High."[6] I imagine that we need to be reminded of that regularly.

So, Daniel 1 begins with tragic new but ends with hope, even though the heroes of the book find themselves in a foreign land. Daniel tells us that God made the four young men who were practicing short-term vegetarianism smart and wise. They read a lot of books and became well-educated. As we explored in the last chapter, what these four young men were learning was not going to be found in the laws of Moses or the writings of any Hebrew scholar. They were learning about the god Marduk and about what it meant to be a Babylonian.

What we understand about these four young men was that they were not letting that knowledge change them. Although they lived into the opportunity to become a part of Nebuchadnezzar's royal court, they were not living into the temptation to let the one true God be pushed out of their hearts and minds. For them, and I think us, learning about another culture or religion or anything else does not automatically equal turning our backs on God.

Dr. Sinclair Ferguson wrote, "The godly may master and employ the learning of the ungodly."[7] Learning about other things, as

---

6   Widder. *Daniel*. Zondervan, 2016. 8.
7   Ferguson. *New Bible Commentary: 21st Century Edition*. InterVarsity Press, 1994. 750.

Daniel and his friends did, may serve as the bridge that allows us to cross over into whatever greater work God has for us. It may allow us to cross over into different contexts and cultures and allow us to provide a powerful witness for God's love for all people.

Not only did the four young men become educated. Daniel could also tell the meaning of dreams and visions. As we all know, this ability served him well throughout the book. This ability, wisdom, or insight to know what someone had dreamed and to be able to decipher the dream came from God and served as part of the bridge that allowed Daniel to cross over into the greater work that God had for him. Dr. J. Dwight Pentecost writes, "The fact that God gave Daniel the ability to understand and interpret visions and dreams meant that throughout Nebuchadnezzar's long reign he depended on Daniel for understanding future events, revealed through dreams and visions."[8]

Think about that for a moment. Daniel became valuable, some would even say indispensable, to the king that had taken Daniel's people captive. Daniel and his friends were taken captive, their hometown was leveled, they were separated from their family and friends, at least for three years, and they were forced to assimilate to the culture of their captors.

Before it was all said and done, Daniel and his friends were promoted several times and eventually became the most trusted advisors to the king that caused all the hurt and pain in the first place. Daniel even outlived King Nebuchadnezzar and eventually became the most trusted advisor to the next king. There seems to be a point to the author of Daniel sharing this information at the end of chapter 1. Dr. Ferguson writes,

> The point is that Daniel lived to see the actions of Nebuchadnezzar reversed. When the king of Babylon was long dead, God's servant continued to live, and his people were restored. Thus, we are prepared for the conflict narratives which follow

8 Pentecost. *The Bible Knowledge Commentary: An Exposition of the Scriptures.* Victor Books, 1985. 1332.

and for the book's visions of the final triumph of the kingdom of God.[9]

As Daniel 1 closes, it seems that, through it all, Daniel and his friends never lost faith in God's sovereignty. They never stopped believing that God was in control. In response, God never stopped using them.

So, what's the point, Terrell? I began this book thinking about the fact that we all experience relationships with people who are not on the same page as us. We all will have to interact with people, and sometimes even be subject to, people whose worldview is completely different from ours. That is one of the realities of being human. But, these relationships with people who are different from us are not always bad. They may feel like an inconvenience for us, but sometimes they serve a greater purpose. I will never claim to know the purposes God has for you and your personal relationships. That's something you will have to pray about and seek God's face to understand.

Not all relationships serve some grand world, community, or life-altering purpose. Sometimes these relationships simply serve as an opportunity for us to share God's love with someone who may not understand what God's love looks like in tangible ways. Other times, participation in these types of relationships may be an opportunity for us to practice what we say we believe in. Daniel and friends lived in a land that was not their own, served in a government that had overtaken theirs and were expected to wholeheartedly buy into a new culture. Although most of us will never experience anything as extreme in our lives, we can still experience the encouragement the author of Daniel likely hoped readers would have.

We can remember God's sovereignty from generation to generation and be encouraged to trust in God's sovereignty and to embrace as our own the hope of past generations. In doing that,

---

9 Ferguson. *New Bible Commentary: 21st Century Edition.* InterVarsity Press, 1994. 750.

we will live into a hopeful mantra that I came across from Dr. W. Sibley Towner who said that when we find ourselves in difficult relationships like Daniel, we should, "Live vigorously, carry your trust into the very heartland of your oppressors, with God's help beat them at their own games of wisdom and understanding, contribute significantly to the safety of your people, and glorify God in your faithfulness."[10]

10 Towner. *Daniel.* John Knox Press, 2012. 28.

An Unanticipated Recognition of God's Sovereignty

Daniel 2

Daniel 2 brings to the surface an important truth related to God's sovereignty. The truth it surfaces is that God reveals God's power and authority in strange ways and at what may seem like the strangest times, and God wants to reveal that truth to everyone. In saying that, I recognize that, as believers in God, this is not a new truth for us. We follow God because we believe in God's sovereignty and power. But, before I go too far, I want to ask a few questions related to our common belief in God's power.

How long have you believed in God and God's authority? Has it been for many years or only a few? What brought you to the place of believing in God's authority? What brought you to faith in God and God's Son as your redeemer? Was it because you were raised in a Christian family and you were taught to believe in God since you were knee high to a grasshopper? Or was your faith brought about due to something you experienced on your own? Was it brought about by your personal experience of God doing something for you that you could not do for yourself?

I ask these questions because we may not think about our conversion experience very often. We know that we have faith in God and sometimes assume that other people should hold the same faith as us and hold it to the same degree that we do without recognizing that their life experiences may be different from ours. Their personal foundations are different from ours and they may not have been raised in a community of faith like many of us were. Because of this, they may see it less as not trusting God

23

and more about getting along as well as they can considering their experiences.

Let me make sure that you understand what I'm trying to convey. I believe that all people should actively be seeking to be in relationship with God. But not everyone has come to a point where they understand that. The fact that they have not yet surrendered their lives to God is not always because they simply want to be stubborn, although that sometimes is the reason. Sometimes they have not surrendered themselves to God because they do not understand who God is or what it means to be in relationship with the truly sovereign Creator of all that is.

I think that Daniel 2 addresses the idea that God sometimes chooses unique methods and means to reveal God's desires to be in relationship with all people and that God has unique plans for everyone, even those who have not yet come to faith. I think this is revealed through six distinct movements or sections in Daniel 2. The first section is found in verses 1-9 where the author of the book reveals that King Nebuchadnezzar had a unique dream that caused him to experience multiple nights of sleeplessness. In the context where the events in the book of Daniel occurred, dreams held great power and were thought to be coded messages from the gods for the person having the dream or for the people group the dreamer belonged to. And if the dreamer was the king or a person with power, it was believed a dream meant something specifically related to their reign or the future of their kingdom.

Due to this belief, dream interpretation was serious business. Kings employed people whose sole purpose was to understand and interpret dreams and visions. Kingdoms like Babylon and Egypt kept track of dreams and their interpretations. They even maintained detailed manuals that were passed along from ruler to ruler and generation to generation so kings and magicians, enchanters, sorcerers, Chaldeans, astrologers, counselors, advisors, and wise men, or whatever your favorite translation of the Bible calls them, could be prepared to respond to the dreaming person with an interpretation.

When the king called his advisors together about his dream, they all likely thought they would be ready to fulfill the king's request. But the king threw them a curve ball. He refused to tell them the dream he had. Instead, he wanted them to tell him his dream and its interpretation. If they could not, they would all die. Understandably, the king's advisors were terrified in the second section of the text. "How can we tell you the dream if we did not have it? The gods will have to give us all the same dream they gave you for us to do what you want. That's virtually impossible because they do not live down here with us and they do not operate in that manner."

This response by the king's advisors acknowledges the real question they were all facing. Who was sovereign? The gods of the Babylonians or a different god? The god that was able to provide the wise men with the answer to the king's question would be recognized and understood as the god with all the power. That god would be the one who not only held the real power, but would also be recognized as the true giver of the dream and the interpretation of the dream would be the true interpretation that would be followed, not only by the king, but by everyone in the kingdom.

As motivation for the wise men, the king decreed that if, by a certain date, the wise men were unable to tell him what his dream had been, they all would be executed. Every one of them would die, including Daniel, his friends, and anyone else who had been elevated to positions as wise men in the royal court. How do you like that for managerial motivation? You would think the king did not trust his advisors. In the third section of the story, Daniel, after hearing the king's decree, asked for an extension to the king's deadline. In asking for an extension, Daniel again showed a certain level of faith in God's sovereignty. The king was already in a tizzy because he did not trust his advisors to be able to do what he asked. How much angrier would he become when one of those advisors asked for an extension on his command?

This is the second time Daniel willingly placed himself in danger of experiencing the king's wrath because he did not want to do as the king had commanded. The first time was when he pushed back against eating the food the king had set aside for them that had been offered to foreign gods. This time, he did it to ask his God for help in knowing what the king had dreamt. In the fourth section of Daniel 2, instead of consulting with the other wise men from Babylon, Daniel called his friends together for prayer. Daniel trusted and believed that God would do what he asked, and he was willing to delay fulfilling the king's request because of his faith in God's ability.

Ultimately, God honored the faithful prayers of Daniel and his friends by revealing to Daniel not only the king's dream but what the dream meant. Daniel rushed to reveal this to the king so that his life, the lives of his friends, and the lives of the Babylonian wise men would be spared. God's revelatory act was not only a response to faithful prayer. It was also an act of confirming that God was the one true God. Dr. Wendy Widder writes, "That he (Daniel) knows the dream at all will testify that the God of heaven—not the Babylonian gods—is the true source of wisdom. And the dream's meaning will proclaim that his (Daniel's) God is also the true source of power, the only one who raises up and takes down human kings."[11]

In the fifth section of the passage, Daniel told the king what the dream was and what it meant. The king had dreamt about a huge statue that was made of multiple materials. Its head was made of gold, its chest and arms were made of silver, its torso (stomach to knees) were made of bronze, its shins and ankles were made of iron, and its feet were a mixture of iron and clay.

I want to pause for a moment and say that this type of dream or imagery was not uncommon in Daniel's context. Other rulers had dreamed of similar images before. There are other histories of kings who had dreamt of this type of statue. What was different

---

11 Widder. *Daniel*. Zondervan, 2016. 50.

about Nebuchadnezzar's dream in Daniel was what came next. As the multi-material statue stood in splendor, a stone was mysteriously cut from a mountain by an unknown person. The stone then struck the feet of the statue destroying the feet. The stone was then used to destroy every other part of the statue. What had been a splendid statue was turned into rubble and was then blown away by the wind. That stone then grew into a mountain that filled the entire earth.

The point of the dream, Daniel said, was that the king, who was typically addressed as the "One who would live forever," would not live forever and neither would his kingdom. Although he was in power presently, a day would come when he would be replaced by another king and kingdom. But that would not be the end. The king and kingdom that replaced him would also be replaced by another power. And that king and kingdom would be replaced. And eventually, that king and kingdom would also be replaced.

When we read this passage or when people preach or teach about this passage, they typically spend considerable time trying to figure out exactly who the succeeding kingdoms were. They also try to find the special meanings behind the materials that made up the statue. When we focus on those things, we miss the main point of the dream. The point of the dream was that kings and kingdoms come and go, including Nebuchadnezzar and Babylon. All human kings and kingdoms have an appointed time to rise and fall. But God's kingdom, represented by the rock that turned into a mountain and destroyed the statue, will replace them all. The one true God's kingship and kingdom, which is not made by human hands, will be the only kingdom that will last forever. God's kingship will be the only one that will never end. God's reign will never come to an end.

Rocks regularly served as imagery that represented God's power and God's desire to be in relationship with the Hebrew people and to protect them throughout the Old Testament. In the psalms, rocks were regularly used to describe God's faithfulness. Psalm 18 says, "You are my mighty rock, my fortress, my protector, the rock where I am safe, my shield, my powerful weapon, and my place of shelter." "You alone are God. Only you are a mighty rock." "You are the living LORD! I will praise you. You are a mighty rock. I will honor you for keeping me safe."

Psalm 31:2-3 says, "Listen to my prayer and hurry to save me. Be my mighty rock and the fortress where I am safe. You, LORD God, are my mighty rock and my fortress. Lead me and guide me, so that your name will be honored." The point of the king's dream was that God, the unbreakable rock, would be the everlasting king ruling over an everlasting kingdom that would be around after King Nebuchadnezzar and Babylon were nothing but memories found in history textbooks.

In the final section of Daniel 2, the king responded to Daniel's words in a way that was unexpected. He worshipped Daniel for his wisdom, showered him with multiple gifts, and promoted Daniel to governor of the area, as well as the head of all the wise men within the kingdom. Daniel's friends were also promoted along with him. More important than that, the king acknowledged that Daniel's God, Jehovah, the one true God, was more powerful than the gods he previously worshipped. He recognized God's sovereignty and worshipped God as the one true God.

As I previously stated, there are multiple similarities between Daniel and Joseph in Genesis. Both men found themselves serving foreign kings who did not trust in their God. Both men were eventually called upon to interpret the dreams of a king when no one else could. And based on God allowing them to interpret those dreams, both men were entrusted with great responsibility that eventually allowed them to help save not only themselves but their people, as well. Both men were used in God's plans to serve and save entire communities.

Of these similarities, Dr. Sharon Pace says, "These two faithful men, both exiles from their homeland, see God working through them. Their ability to interpret dreams is ancillary to their true gift:

the ability to look at terrible things that happen to them or their people and still see that they are part of God's plan for good."[12] I recognize that this whole story seems like it is about the king and his unexpected recognition of God's sovereignty, but I think that the point is bigger than that. I think the dream and its interpretation were not primarily for the king, but for the people who would one day hear about it.

Although the king had the dream, and the interpretation of the dream had consequences for him, I think the dream and its interpretation were really meant for the dream interpreter and his people so they could have hope. God gave Daniel the answer to the king's dream so he and his people could have hope in a land where it seemed like hope could not be found. Dr. Pace continues,

> The dream tells the reader that the world follows God's plan, precisely at a time when people may have every reason to doubt that history has any meaning. Even the tyrants exist because they serve God's will, and Nebuchadnezzar only has power over a defeated people because God permits it.[13]

Even during the hardest moments of life, God still reminded God's people that God had not forgotten about them. The same rings true for us today. Circumstances may seem unchangeable but God's love, power, and authority in our lives will eventually overcome everything that life throws at us. We should not forget this. Amen.

12 Pace. *Daniel*. Smyth & Helwys, 2008. 81.
13 Ibid. 82.

Finding Protection
Within God's Sovereignty

DANIEL 3

As I have studied the book of Daniel, I've come to realize that every chapter and section of verses within the book introduces an important truth related to God's sovereignty. The first section of Daniel introduced the overall idea that God is sovereign over and against all other powers and principalities. The third section explored the idea that people will sometimes recognize God's power after experiencing it firsthand. The third section explored the idea that God, in God's sovereignty, sometimes both allows and intentionally uses unanticipated relationships to accomplish God's holy desires.

Daniel 3 introduces us to a truth that I must acknowledge I find uncomfortable and frustrating. That truth is that pain, discomfort, and inconvenience often play a part in God showing the world and Christians that God is, and that God is sovereign. In the process of God showing kings and dictators that their power is limited, verifying that God can change what others have declared as unchangeable, and God showing that God's authority surpasses the authority of all other power in creation, pain may be involved. The fact that pain somehow plays a part in all our lives has been a part of philosophical and ethics discussions about God, God's existence, and God's sovereignty since people first began to discuss and debate God's existence and authority.

Inevitably, secular philosophical and ethics discussions push back against the idea of an all-powerful and loving God even being possible because evil and pain exist so prominently in the world. Philosophers

have been unable to get away from the challenge of an all-powerful God allowing pain to exist, let alone thinking that God may use pain as part of a holy process.

Believers in God are not off the hook as it relates to discussions of God's power and authority amid the existence of pain and discomfort. When believers place their trust in God, that does not free us from pain, inconvenience, or disappointment in our lives. If given the chance, many of us could probably say that pain seems to be one of the constants that accompany our relationship with God. I've met people who have told me that they did not know what pain was until they placed their trust in God.

In his book *The Problem of Pain*, C. S. Lewis attempts to address the question of why a loving God would allow evil to exist in the world. Mr. Lewis frames the common challenge believers and nonbelievers face this way:

> If God were good, He would make His creatures perfectly happy, and if He were almighty, He would be able to do what he wished. But the creatures are not happy (and some would add they often are not safe). Therefore, God lacks either goodness, or power, or both.[14]

Ms. Lewis' words are the epitome of what it means to struggle with the idea of evil.

In Daniel 3, Daniel's friends, Shadrach, Meshach, and Abednego experienced the daunting challenge of facing evil and its implications on their lives. It's believed that 19 years had passed between Daniel chapter 2, which we explored in the last chapter, and chapter 3. In chapter 2, King Nebuchadnezzar learned that God was sovereign by miraculously showing Daniel the dream the king had and giving Daniel the interpretation for the dream. The king praised Daniel and Daniel's God for this revelation. But, 19 years later in chapter 3, it seemed that the king had forgotten all that he had learned about God's power in chapter 2.

---

14 Lewis. *The Problem of Pain*. Harper One, 1996. 16.

As chapter 3 began, we learn that the king had erected a statue made of gold on the plains of the Dura Valley and called all his officials from various places to come see it. We do not know exactly what the statue was or what it represented. It may have been an idol representing one of the gods worshipped in Babylon or it could have been an image that represented King Nebuchadnezzar. The overall problem with this scene was not necessarily that everyone who stood before it was expected to bow before it. I know this will sound strange to hear, but technically, there was no rule in God's word that prohibited God's followers from bowing to a king out of respect or bowing at any time as a sign of respect.

The problem was that the king was not asking those present to bow out of respect. He was asking them to bow out of allegiance. Allegiance to what the statue represented. This was the evil that manifested itself in the lives of the three followers of God. If they did not bow to the image, their lives would be forfeited. The people present were being asked to either show allegiance to the god the statue represented or allegiance to the king it represented or lose their lives.

Neither option was very acceptable to anyone who followed Daniel's God, the one true God. Although respect could be shown to anyone who deserved it, allegiance was to be given only to God. This is one of the challenges that all of us will face as we seek to "live" in the world but not be "of" the world. How do we, like Shadrach, Meshach, and Abednego, live into the opportunities to occupy positions within the king's royal courts without giving in to the pressures to give our allegiance to the positions we occupy or give allegiance to the ones who give us those positions?

Apparently, other people within the king's court understood the dilemma the three men faced because they were actively looking for the men to refuse to bow to the image. When the men did not bow, the onlookers reported them to the king. This was the second inconvenience that the three men faced. It seemed as if those who reported the three men had been waiting for the opportunity to make their lives miserable and jumped at the opportunity to see them punished for not bowing to the image. As the students at the university where I work say, "Haters gon' hate!" My grandmother would say that evil never rests and it is always looking for a reason or way to get at you.

After hearing about their failure to bow to the image, the king gave the three men another opportunity to show their allegiance by bowing. If they refused to comply, they would be thrown into a furnace and burned alive. They refused his offer. Their refusal to comply with his order is interesting and raises another truth that I think should be acknowledged as part of the larger conversation about evil and God's sovereign ability to deliver God's followers from the power of evil. That truth is that they were willing to be obedient even though they had no guarantee that God would save them.

In the Contemporary English Version, the king said,

> I hear that you refuse to worship my gods and the gold statue I have set up. Now I am going to give you one more chance. If you bow down and worship the statue when you hear the music, everything will be all right. But if you do not, you will at once be thrown into a flaming furnace. No god can save you from me.

The king's confidence in himself is the third instance of evil pushing against the three men.

The three men responded, "Our Majesty, we do not need to defend ourselves. The God we worship can save us from you and your flaming furnace. But even if he doesn't, we still won't worship your gods and the gold statue you have set up." The Message Bible says it in a way that I really appreciate. "Your threat means nothing to us. If you throw us in the fire, the God we serve can rescue us from your roaring furnace and anything else you might cook up, O king. But even if he does not, it would not make a bit of difference, O king. We still would not serve your gods or worship the gold statue you set up."

The three men determined to do what God wanted, regardless of the consequences. They believed that God could save them from any punishment the king could order for them. But there was no guarantee that God would save them. Their faith in God and determination to do what was right was not predicated on them receiving a promise that God would keep them from experiencing the consequences of their decision, even though their decision to not bow was righteous. They were willing to do the right thing, even if it led to them experiencing pain. Dr. Wendy Widder frames the dilemma faced by the men this way, "The three men believed their God was able to deliver them from the furnace, therefore they would not bow before any other god. Whether their God would deliver them was another matter, but he most certainly was able."[15]

The men knew God could do what they needed. In Daniel chapter 2, we learned that they were the ones who prayed with Daniel that God would miraculously reveal the king's dream and God answered their prayers. I imagine they each had other personal examples of God proving God's strength and capability in their lives. God's power and ability were never in doubt. What could have been in doubt was God's willingness to act on this occasion.

But, if God decided not to deliver them, they would remain faithful to what they believed God wanted from them. They were never guaranteed that God would deliver them from the evil that wanted to harm them or reward them for their faith. Yet, they remained faithful. This is another primary challenge we all still face today. The challenge to do what is right in God's sight even if that right decision leads to us experiencing the power or consequences of evil actions in our lives.

Fortunately for the three men, God did deliver them. After the king had them thrown into the furnace, the king was the first person to notice that they were walking around in the furnace, unharmed. Not only were the three men walking around unharmed, there was a mysterious fourth person in the furnace with them. The

15 Widder. *Daniel.* Zondervan, 2016. 72.

king described this fourth person as someone who looked like a god, or looked like one of the sons of God, or looked like the Son of God. Understandably, a lot is made of who this fourth person could have been.

The Aramaic phrase that is used to describe the appearance of this fourth person (a son of God or a son of the gods) is a general reference to spiritual beings that were sent by God for a task. It's the same language and idea that was found in Job 1:6 where the writer describes the "sons of God" that were in heaven meeting with God. As exciting as it is to read about a person walking in the furnace with the men, the primary focus of the story is not on the person in the furnace but is instead on the fact that God delivered the men and blessed them for their faithfulness. Dr. Widder says it this way, "Whether the fourth figure was God himself or just his angel, God is the one delivering his servants from the king's hand."[16]

In Daniel 3, the three men faced multiple instances of evil arising in their lives and challenging them to give allegiance to something other than God. Their faith and dedication to God were what caused them to experience the challenge of evil to their faith in the first place. And, although they never had a guarantee that God would act miraculously on their behalf, their love for God, and their desire to be obedient to God's wishes caused them to remain faithful to their allegiance to God, even in the face of certain pain and suffering. The truth that is revealed to us in Daniel 3 is that faithful living does not necessarily equal easy living or drama-free living for God's followers. The opposite may be true. The more faithfully we live, the more we may be brought to the attention of people who do not value our faithfulness to God. These people may become the embodiment of evil in our lives.

Dr. Widder writes,

> In a bit of biblical irony, Shadrach, Meshach, and Abed-nego heeded the ages past admonition of Moses never to worship any form of any god (or God) because their God was

---

16 Ibid. 75.

a consuming fire, yet the price the three men paid for their obedience was being cast into a raging fire. But the fire to be feared was never that of foreign oppressors. The only fire to fear was the consuming fire of their God. And just as God had once delivered Israelites from the iron-smelting furnace of Egyptian bondage, so he delivered their descendants from the furnace of blazing fire when, trapped in a land of idolatry, they gave him their exclusive worship.[17]

At some point, I think we all have faced or will face the fiery furnace of the certainty of evil and the uncertainty of how God will respond. Like Shadrach, Meshach, and Abednego, we can determine to follow God's will even when the ending is not fully clear about how God will respond. That type of faithfulness is never easy, but it is the type of faithfulness God seeks from us.

---

17 Ibid. 74.

God as Sovereign Kingmaker and Kingbreaker

DANIEL 4

The book of Daniel reveals many truths about God's sovereignty that are beneficial and difficult to its readers. These truths are beneficial and difficult not only for God's children but also for those who find themselves outside God's family. Some of the truths we have learned so far in Daniel have been encouraging, hope-building, and awe-inspiring. Yet, on the opposite side, some of the truths, like the one we will learn momentarily, are frustrating and can cause us to scratch our heads because we may not fully understand why God does what God does.

To get directly to the point, the truth that is found in Daniel 4 is that in God's sovereignty, God will elevate some people to positions of power, authority, or influence over others, even when we do not think that person should be in that position. Ultimately, we should not fret because, in God's sovereignty, God can also demote and take authority away from people who are in power when their lives and actions do not align with God's wishes. This is the lesson that King Nebuchadnezzar, the feared and revered king of Babylon, learned at great expense to himself and his legacy in Daniel 4.

Chapter 4 is especially unique in the overall book of Daniel, and the Bible, because it is the only chapter of the Bible that seems to tell a story from the vantage point of someone outside of the family of God. It reads as a firsthand account of one unique experience of King Nebuchadnezzar. Daniel 4 begins by stating that it was a letter written by the king that was sent out to all people in the world so they could know and

understand the signs, wonders, and sovereignty of Daniel's God and God's kingdom. He wrote this portion of Daniel so that all people would praise Daniel's God as the sovereign Creator as the king had.

Why was King Nebuchadnezzar proclaiming God's signs, wonders, and sovereignty this time? Because the king had experienced another life-changing, God-affirming dream. In the king's first dream from Daniel 2, the king saw a huge statue composed of various metals standing on a plain. The head of that statue was made of gold. That gold portion of the statue represented King Nebuchadnezzar's rule as the mightiest king at that time. Through the dream and its interpretation by Daniel, the king learned that, after his death, the mighty kingdom of Babylon, and the king's legacy, would eventually be divided into smaller and weaker governments. Those governments would eventually be replaced by the kingdom and work of Daniel's God.

The king took this news in stride and recognized Daniel's God as the one true God. As we learned in the last chapter, this change to acknowledging Daniel's God lasted somewhere around 19 years. But, one problem arose after that first dream. It seemed like the king could not shake the image he had from that first dream because he eventually had a huge golden statue, like the one from his dream, built on a nearby plain. That statue represented his kingdom and he required all his subordinates to bow before that statute.

Daniel's friends, Shadrach, Meshach, and Abednego refused the king's orders to bow. Although the king had them thrown into a fiery furnace for their disobedience, God stepped in and saved the three men from physical harm. After that miraculous event, the king, again, saw the error of his ways and acknowledged God as the true king. This seemed to be the cyclical habit of King Nebuchadnezzar. He would do something to declare himself as the one true king that was to be envied, only to find out through a dream, miracle, or show of power from Daniel's God that Daniels's God was the one true king.

Multiple times God caused the king to have strange dreams as a way for God to tell him that he and the false gods he served were not as mighty as he thought. Despite Nebuchadnezzar's position as king, and his success as the conqueror of multiple nations, Daniel's God was the mightiest of all, and Daniel's God was the only one who should be worshipped. Unfortunately, the king never seemed to fully learn this lesson. He would repent and change his ways for a short time, but he would eventually do something stupid, again, only to have Daniel's God remind him that his rule was only temporary. This is what occurred through the dream and its interpretation in Daniel 4.

Instead of a multi-material statue in this dream, King Nebuchadnezzar dreamed about a tree that stood in the center of the world. The tree was so large that it reached up to the heavens and could be seen by anyone in the world. The tree also provided protection and food for all the people and animals in the world. The tree was a good thing that did good things for the world. The king's dream of a tree that reached the heavens and provided fruit for the world was not out of the ordinary. There were other stories of kings that had dreamt about trees and being turned into trees. Trees were symbolic of multiple things in that culture including their importance for providing for communities. Kings were also viewed as holy trees.

Trees and kings regularly served as symbols linking the connections between the heavens and the earth or the dwelling places of the gods and the dwelling place of humans. Trees were understood to be sources of protection and sustenance for people and communities. Kings were often referred to as trees because their positions as rulers over people symbolized their holy responsibilities as leaders which were given to them by the gods to protect and provide for those whom they ruled over.

But there is a strange aspect to the king's dream. The dream ended with an angel coming down from heaven and commanding that the tree be cut down to its stump. Its branches and fruit were to be scattered throughout the world and the stump and its roots were to remain in the ground. The stump would stay in the ground unprotected, bound by chains, and covered in dew. As you would expect, there were unique implications for King Nebuchadnezzar in this dream.

Daniel told him that the dream was an indictment against the king because the king had gotten too big for his britches and had placed too much faith in himself and the false gods he served. King Nebuchadnezzar believed that he was successful as king because of his own power and wisdom and the protection of other gods. What he did not understand was that all his success had come from Daniel's God. He had his kingdom, wealth, and power because Daniel's God had given it to him.

The king was the tree in the dream. Vast, powerful, and protecting, his reach and influence could not be ignored. But he had to stop thinking that what he achieved came from his own abilities. Like the dream in Daniel 2, the dream in Daniel 4 was a warning that God was paying attention to the king and would change things in a negative way if the king did not change his ways and fully acknowledge God's power. As the statue in Daniel 2 was destroyed and swept away in the wind, the tree in Daniel 4 would experience a similar fate.

I want to pause for a moment and look at an interesting aspect of the conversation between Daniel and the king as they talked about the dream. Their conversation about the dream occurred in Daniel 4:19-27, which we did not read. The thing that jumped out at me about that section was how caring Daniel was when he explained the dream and what it meant for the king. Daniel, who had been taken as a prisoner of the king, and removed from his homeland by the king, did not celebrate at the king's potential demise after God revealed the meaning of the dream to him.

Daniel did not rub the implications of the dream in the king's face. He did not say "This is what you get for taking me and my friends prisoner and destroying our city." He did not say, "I cannot wait to see your kingdom end." Instead, he spoke compassionately to the king, almost like he felt sorry for the king. Daniel's remedy for the king not to experience God's punishment was two-fold. The king should acknowledge God as the true sovereign ruler and do what was right in God's sight.

Different translations say it in multiple ways. Practice righteousness to the poor, show mercy to the oppressed (English Standard Version), have mercy on those who were mistreated (Contemporary English Version), or look at the needs of the down and out (The Message Bible). Daniel's suggestion to the king to be able to avoid God's judgment was to change his ways and begin to look out for those who could not look out for themselves. In doing this, God would know that his heart was truly changed, and God would change God's mind about punishing him.

Unfortunately, the king failed to heed Daniel's advice. Less than a year later, the king was walking on the roof of his palace when he gloated and gloried in the expansiveness of his kingdom. Daniel 4:30 says that before the king could get his egotistical words out of his mouth, a voice from heaven declared that he had not learned the lessons from the multiple dreams God sent him. Because of his failure to heed God's warning, the king would be driven mad and he would begin to act like a wild beast, roam the wilderness with other animals eating grass, and no longer acting human.

The king would go crazy. It really did not matter what psychological condition the king would experience. What was important was the fact that God was going to punish him for his egotistical thinking and actions. Dr. Widder writes,

> The exact nature of the king's illness is not the point of the narrative, which is far more interested in theological matters. The greatest king of the day is about to be transformed into a beast for thinking himself to be a god. When a mighty man blurred the lines between humanity and divinity, the Divine judged him by blurring the lines between humanity and sub-humanity.[18]

18 Ibid. 95.

The king experienced a season of madness where he roamed the wilderness, unshaven with long fingernails, eating grass, and waking up every day covered with the morning dew. Scholars believe he experienced an extended episode of Boanthropy, a psychological disorder that causes a person to believe they are a cow or ox. The king remained in this state until one day he came to his senses, repented, and acknowledged that God was the sovereign kingmaker and king breaker. When he finally repented, God restored his sanity and his kingdom.

I cannot read this story without having multiple questions that any honest reader of Daniel would likely have. What did Daniel mean when he told the king that God was the one who set rulers in their place? Does that mean that God elevates or allows evil rulers to rise to the top? What does it mean for God to tell the king multiple times that his kingdom was made possible only by God? Did God forget that the king destroyed the holy city that God had given to God's people as a gift and took God's people as captives? Why did God remove the king, whom many would call evil, only to restore him back to power later? Would it not have made more sense to let the punishment stand so Judah could be set free and a king chosen from God's people could replace him?

The book of Daniel does not answer these questions. Instead, the truth that Daniel shares in Daniel 4 is that God does allow or cause some people to come to power that we think do not deserve to be in power. In holy sovereignty, God lifts some whom we think should not be lifted. In God's sovereignty, God will elevate and demote whom God chooses to. Daniel 4 leaves us with the nagging question, "What are we to do when this happens?" This is not a hypothetical question. I think it is one that we all can recognize as relevant today in our nation and in our personal lives.

If I asked how many readers have ever worked for or with someone who did not deserve the position they held, we all could likely say we knew someone who fit that description. We can all name someone who held a position of power or authority whom we thought either abused their power or did not deserve to occupy their position. I think the lesson for us as we think about the truth that God elevates and demotes whom God chooses, is found in the actions of Daniel as he explained the meaning of the king's dream. Daniel did not see the king's demise as a thing to be celebrated. Instead, he saw it as a tragic thing.

Daniel understood that God had placed and kept the king in his position. Daniel did not need to understand why. He only needed to know that God was involved in keeping the king in power. If, and when, God wanted things to change, God would bring about change in a way that no one could stand against. It was Daniel's job to remain faithful to what he understood as God's desires for his own life as he served in the king's court. The same holds true for us today. When we understand the idea that God is in control of everything, the elevation of someone we do not agree with may not make us happy, but that elevation will not cause us to lose faith in God's sovereignty. And the recognition of God's sovereignty should cause us to trust that God has a plan and that plan will ultimately come to fruition, even if that plan means people we do not like gain certain positions.

As we experience the tension between living in a world filled with people whom we do not like or trust, may we remember that God is in control and God asks us to trust God's plan and show care and concern for the people that God uses to fulfill that plan. Even the people we do not like or trust that much.

THE DICHOTOMY OF
GOD'S SOVEREIGN MERCY

DANIEL 5

An often overlooked, and I would even say misunderstood, aspect of God's sovereignty is that God does not always show God's strength when we think God should. Have you ever thought that the times God's reputation and God's people would most benefit from a clear and sure sign of God's authority and power seem to be the times when God is quiet or not active? Please understand that question is not a complaint about God or how God acts. It's just an observation that I imagine many of us have made before.

I imagine that there have been occasions in all our lives when we have prayed our hearts out and have exhibited a level of faith we believe could move mountains only to see those mountains still standing when we opened our eyes after saying "Amen." I think that one of the things we learn from the book of Daniel is that many times God is strategic in how and when God shows God's power. Although God is always all-powerful and always capable of moving mountains, God does so according to God's own perfect timing. The story that is told in Daniel 5 is a prime example of this.

Daniel 5 opens with King Belshazzar throwing a feast with his royal court. Belshazzar is the second king of Babylon mentioned in the book of Daniel. He was the son of a king named Nabonidus. Nabonidus came to power after King Nebuchadnezzar. Nabonidus was a cunning and ruthless leader who, after securing his rule over Babylon, spent a lot of time vacationing in the foreign countries he had overtaken. Whenever he was on vacation, his son Belshazzar occupied the throne in his place.

History tells us that at this specific time in Nabonidus' reign and Belshazzar's fill-in leadership, the Persian army, the newest and greatest world power, was marching to the doorstep of Babylon, ready to overtake it. History also tells us that the Persian army had recently gained control of one of the foreign provinces Belshazzar's father ruled and the Persian army was marching towards Babylon to continue overtaking the land of Nabonidus. So, the fill-in king was holding a banquet and getting drunk as his country's greatest enemy at the time was marching towards them, anticipating another victory.

Banquets in the Hebrew Bible were not an arbitrary occurrence. They usually were held for a specific meaning. They were usually held in conjunction with something important to the people or person that was experiencing them. When we read about someone outside of God's family holding one, it often meant they were celebrating something that was in opposition to God or God's people. It could be a feast in honor of a false god that was in competition with God or to recognize a victory someone believed their god gave them over someone else. If a banquet was being held by someone outside God's family, it was usually related to that person or people trying to express their power or privilege over and against God or God's people.

Daniel does not tell us specifically what feast was being celebrated or why the wine was flowing, but scholars have multiple ideas of what could have been occurring that caused the king to open the taps on the royal liquor cabinet. Belshazzar may have been celebrating the New Year festival related to the worship of the god Sin, the god his father King Nabonidus followed. I imagine the writer of Daniel probably thought about this irony as they were composing this story about Belshazzar.

Another theory is that Belshazzar knew that his enemies had just overtaken one of their cities and were on the way to Babylon to continue their expansion. In response to the approaching enemy, Belshazzar may have thrown a banquet to raise the spirits of his royal court and to distract them from their impending defeat. A further theory was that the banquet was Belshazzar's way of worshipping the god Sin in the hopes that this god would rescue them from coming defeat. It was his way to say that he remembered the past victories he believed his father's god had given them and to toast the false god Sin so Sin would step in on their behalf again.

To remind the false god Sin of prior victories over other gods, Belshazzar ordered that religious relics of the last major god that had been defeated by Babylon be brought out from the temple. The last major god they believed had been defeated by Babylon was the God of Daniel. Since Daniel's God did not allow images to be made representing God's image, the only religious relics Nebuchadnezzar could take from the temple in Jerusalem when he defeated Judah were gold and silver vessels. History tells us that these items which had been taken by Nebuchadnezzar had been in Babylon's temple for 47 years.

So, for 47 years, the items that represented Daniel's God had sat in a foreign temple. For 47 years, the images that best physically represented the power of Daniel's God had been in Babylon's temple sitting at the feet of another god. And for some reason, Belshazzar thought it would be a good idea to not only bring them out but to use them as part of his efforts to call upon a false god to ask for help in protecting Babylon from a coming fight.

In sharing the king's actions of calling for and using vessels dedicated to Daniel's God in this feast, the writer of Daniel reveals two things that were of the utmost importance for God's children who were still in captivity and wondering where God was and why God had not done something substantial to free them from their enemies. First, the writer was revealing that Belshazzar was about to find out that this move was not only a bad idea, but he was going to learn that the God he believed had been defeated by King Nebuchadnezzar was actually alive and well and ready to do something in response to the disrespect he was being shown. Essentially, the writer was reminding the readers that God had not been defeated. God was still around, God was still all-powerful, and God was still involved.

Second, the items from Jerusalem's temple were symbols of the God Daniel served. The appearance of these items would serve as a reminder of the hope that had been wrapped up in them before they had been taken by Nebuchadnezzar. They represented the return of hope that accompanied the return of God's presence for God's children. Finding out that these items were being brought out into the open would have been like the music that is typically played in a movie right before the hero appears to win the final battle. The 'defeated' God whom everyone believed was sleeping or in hibernation was in a sense waking up and reemerging on the scene ready to win a decisive victory.

In response to Belshazzar's acts of disrespect, a mysterious disembodied hand suddenly emerged out of nowhere near the king and began to write a message on the wall. This ghostly hand represented judgment against the king. A severed hand was a sign that someone had been defeated or killed in battle. To keep an accurate count of how many people had been killed during a battle, the side that won would cut off the right hand of every dead enemy and tally them. They would also use the severed hands as propaganda tools to intimidate survivors of battle or other enemies.

Daniel's God, whom Belshazzar thought was dead, used the symbol Belshazzar and his father likely used during their battles as the symbol to show him that his defeat was near. God sometimes has an interesting sense of humor. As Belshazzar looked on in amazement, the severed hand wrote three brief words on a wall. The words were the equivalent of the following based on various translations: Numbered, Weighed, and Divided or Numbered, Counted, and Measured.

As was true during Nebuchadnezzar's reign, the king's wise men could not understand what the words were, let alone what they meant. The king's mother had to tell him to go find Daniel because he was the only one in the kingdom who could understand what was going on when strange things like this occurred. Daniel, who was likely an old man at this time shared the meaning of the hand-written message. Belshazzar's actions and reign had been judged by the one true God and the judgment was not good for the king. His days had been numbered by God, his reign and actions as king had been weighed by God and were found to be sorely wanting, and the kingdom of his father was about to be divided by God between two other kingdoms.

The book of Daniel tells us that those two kingdoms were the kingdoms of the Medes and the Persians. This defeat and division were due to Belshazzar's despicable acts, especially the act of calling on another God while using vessels that represented Daniel's God. Belshazzar lived into the legacy of the kings before him. Instead of trusting in the one true God, he put his trust in false gods. Like King Nebuchadnezzar, enough evidence had been made available to him for him to follow Daniel's God and reap the benefits. Instead, he trusted in a god who would fail him in the hour that he most needed help.

Dr. Widder says the following about the sin that was at the heart of Belshazzar's downfall:

> First, even though the king knew of Nebuchadnezzar's pride, he didn't humble his own heart. Instead he set himself against Yahweh by desecrating his sacred vessels and worshipping idols with them in hand. Finally, he failed to honor God, who provided his every breath.[19]
>
> Daniel's indictment (against Belshazzar) suggest(s) that the main problem with Belshazzar was that he refused to learn from the example of God's judgment on Nebuchadnezzar. Belshazzar was unteachable, and while Nebuchadnezzar may have been a challenging student, he nonetheless learned.[20]

Within a day, Belshazzar learned the same hard lesson King Nebuchadnezzar learned before him. Unfortunately for Belshazzar, he was not given the opportunity to repent as Nebuchadnezzar was

19 Ibid. 116.
20 Ibid. 122.

and he lost his life and kingdom. The dream that Nebuchadnezzar experienced in Daniel 2 about his kingdom being divided into smaller weaker kingdoms was being fulfilled.

I believe there are a few practical truths are reaffirmed by what we learn in Daniel 5 and the debauchery of King Belshazzar. If King Belshazzar were alive today, I imagine he would put the truths this way. First, although it may look like the God of Daniel is defeated, asleep, or unconcerned, the opposite is true. If it seems like the God of Daniel is not paying attention, it is more likely that God is waiting for a specific moment to act and affirm God's holy power. Although it may look like a person or power has gained a victory over God or God's people, the truth is that God can and will act to reaffirm God's power and plan at a time God sees fit.

Second, I imagine the king might say that although it may look like a person or power has gained a victory over God or God's people in the past, there is no guarantee that person or power will maintain power. The opposite is true. Anyone or anything that stands in opposition to God will ultimately be defeated.

Finally, I imagine the king would say that God's process for removing evil may occur quickly or slowly, but evil will ultimately be removed. King Nebuchadnezzar was given the opportunity to repent and turn to the one true God multiple times. King Belshazzar was not even granted that much. The pace at which God removes evil is up to God.

Before I cast too many stones at either Nebuchadnezzar or Belshazzar, I must hold a mirror up to myself. The judgments that were made against both kings were in response to their blatant blasphemies against God. I know the word blasphemy is a word we all probably take seriously, so let me explain what I mean by using it. Dr. Widder defines blasphemy this way. "It is the failure to take God seriously for who he is—that is, who he has revealed himself to be in the pages of Scripture."[21]

---

21 Ibid. 120

If I were to be honest, I must acknowledge that on multiple occasions I have, whether intentionally or unintentionally, not taken God seriously for who God is. Maybe that was due to a lack of faith when I perceived some problem to be bigger than God could handle. Or when I thought I was strong enough on my own to handle something without God's assistance. Like Nebuchadnezzar, God has been gracious and allowed me ample opportunities to repent and turn to the one true God for my salvation and preservation. I imagine the same is true for you. May we remember God's patient preservation before we celebrate the swift demise of unwise kings or other people.

God's Sovereignty
Over Law and Location

DANIEL 6

One of the important aspects of religious faith during Daniel's time was the general belief that, although the gods primarily dwelled in the heavens, they each exhibited control over specific areas of creation. For example, one god was believed to be in control of the sky and the weather. People would pray to that god for good weather or rain if their community had been experiencing a drought. It was believed that another god was in control of the sea and that god would be implored to calm raging waters so sailors could experience peace on a journey.

It was believed that another god was the god of the land in a region and people would request that god make the ground fertile so families could experience the blessing of a bountiful harvest at the end of certain planting seasons. For most communities, they worshipped multiple gods in the hopes that their multiple needs would be met. Most gods were believed to be bound by region or location.

This was not only true for gods. This was true for kings, who were thought to be the sons, or representatives of the gods, or gods themselves. A king was believed to have received their authority from the gods and their reign over a city or kingdom was due to the favor a god or gods had shown them. When they enacted a law or decree, they did it with the full authority and approval of the gods behind them. They and their gods were bound by those laws and decrees.

In Daniel 6, a truth that was unique to Daniel's God was

brought forth. The truth was that Daniel's God was not bound by a region or location or man-made law. God's sovereignty was not bound by physical parameters of geography or legal parameters of decrees or laws. All space belonged to God and all law was subject to God's power. The revelation of this truth began with a conspiracy against Daniel by leaders of the royal court for King Darius, historically known as Darius the Great. Darius was the third king mentioned in Daniel. Darius was a mighty king who quelled multiple rebellions at the beginning of his rule.

One of the early inventions of his reign was to divide his large kingdom into smaller provinces or states. The writer of Daniel tells us that the king divided the kingdom into 120 smaller states, each with a governor. These 120 governors reported to three higher officials with Daniel serving as one of these higher officials. As was Daniel's habit, he worked diligently for the king and served the king well. His reputation was solid, and the king was able to put a lot of trust in Daniel's leadership. The king planned to elevate Daniel even higher due to his trustworthiness.

The favor Daniel found in the eyes of the king did not sit well with the other two officials who served alongside him and they sought out ways to discredit him. The problem for these two other leaders was that Daniel's reputation was impeccable and these two officials knew they would be unable to find any of the typical faults with him. He was not dishonest. He did not do anything to try to bring attention to himself or to build a coalition for himself. The only thing they could try to do to hurt Daniel would have to be related to his faith in his God.

The irony of this idea was that the perception they likely held was that Daniel's God was an ineffective God because Daniel's God, who was believed to be the God of Jerusalem, had been defeated and artifacts dedicated to that God had been taken from the temple in Jerusalem and placed in positions of subjection to the god Marduk in a temple in Babylon. If Daniel's God had been the God of Jerusalem, he was no longer the God of anywhere because

Jerusalem had been destroyed and laid in ruins and the items that had been dedicated to him were stuck in a temple dedicated to another god.

Over time, the people that served Daniel's God experienced the pain of living in subjection to not one, not two, but three separate kings who served multiple gods who were in opposition to their God and whom they believed had taken control of the land where Daniel's God resided. Nebuchadnezzar's god had given him victory over Jerusalem and Judah several years before. Then Nebuchadnezzar's kingdom was overtaken by King Belshazzar's father, King Nabonidus, and they reigned for multiple years until their kingdom was overtaken by King Darius and his god.

Through these multiple exchanges of kingdoms, Daniel's God never seemed to rise to the occasion by freeing the people of Judah and returning them to their homeland. This was evidence to them that Daniel's God was at a minimum ineffective. In the minds of these two leaders, Daniel's God was a nonfactor in daily life. Daniel's God was not one to be feared because he had no land to be God over. What these two leaders likely feared was how Daniel's faith in his God caused him to live in an honorable way that made them look bad. Although Daniel lived in subjection, he still lived in accordance with the things he believed his God wanted for him.

In response to their frustration with how Daniel's faith caused him to live, these two leaders concocted a plan to convince the king to make a law that did not allow anyone to pray to anyone else or any other god other than the king for 30 days. Having his ego stroked, the king bought into this idea, likely not fully thinking it through, and issued a decree that no other god or person was to be prayed to for a month. As you can imagine, Daniel continued to do what he thought his God wanted, even if it meant violating the king's decree. After learning about the new law of the king, Daniel went home and openly prayed towards Jerusalem in front of an open window, which seems to have been his regular practice. The two conspiring leaders saw him praying and went back to tell the king of Daniel's violation of the new law.

I think there are two interesting aspects of Daniel's act of praying at the open window. First, Daniel's act of prayer may have been an intentional act of insubordination. I say this because Daniel could have avoided anyone knowing he was praying by simply doing it in another private place in his home. He could have kept his prayer between him and God without anyone else finding out. Which raises the question, why did he pray at the window?

That is the second interesting aspect. It is believed that there was an oral tradition that Daniel followed that stated that anytime a person prayed to God, they were to face towards the Holy of Holies, the most holy place in the temple where the manifestation of God's presence could be found. In order to face the Holy of Holies, a person had to turn in the direction of Jerusalem.

It seems like Daniel prayed in this way as an act of acknowledging God's ongoing presence, even though the holy city had been destroyed and God may have been quiet for a while. Daniel intentionally prayed facing Jerusalem, the city of God that lay in ruins, to say that he still believed that God was alive and active. By doing this, it seemed that Daniel was acknowledging that Jerusalem was the place where God's presence dwelled. God's space was in Jerusalem. God's presence was in Jerusalem. But, Daniel, Darius, and the other leaders were about to find out that God's presence transcended location and law.

After the two leaders saw Daniel praying, they immediately advised the king of Daniel's disobedience. Due to the belief that the laws he enacted were immutable, and possibly the embarrassment that would have ensued if he tried to change his mind, the king believed he had no choice but to hold Daniel accountable. Accountability meant that Daniel had to be thrown into a pit filled with lions. Darius was distraught over this. He seemed to genuinely be concerned about Daniel and what would happen to him. So much so that the king acknowledged Daniel's faith in his God and the king verbalized the hope that the God Daniel followed would override the king's power and law and save him.

Of this ironic statement by the king, Dr. Joseph de Bruyn says, "Even though Darius may be the embodiment of a god, he does not have the power to rescue or to protect Daniel within his own god space."[22] This is one of the problems with humans who consider themselves to be gods. Their power really is not as grand as they or other people believe. Daniel was thrown into the pit of lions, a stone was secured over the opening of the pit, and the opening was sealed with the king's signet ring as a sign that no one could open the pit for fear of death.

I want to pause for a moment and say that this type of punishment for Daniel was not unique. In Daniel's context, it was called an "ordeal". An ordeal was a common practice for discerning whether a person who had been accused of a crime or wrongdoing was guilty of that crime. If a person was believed to have done something wrong, they were placed into a situation where their innocence for a crime was verified by the god, they followed acting on their behalf to protect them and save their life. If their god saved them, they were innocent. If their god did not save them, they were guilty of what they were accused of.

According to Dr. John H. Walton, "Most trials by ordeal in the ancient Near East involved dangers such as water, fire or poison. When the accused was exposed to these threats, he or she was in effect being assumed guilty until the deity declared otherwise."[23] Daniel's innocence was proven the following day when the king ordered the stone covering the opening to the lion's pit removed and Daniel emerged proclaiming God's protection throughout the night through angels.

Does any of this sound familiar? Daniel's placement into a pit that was covered by a rock, and his subsequent emergence vindicat-

22 De Bruyn. "*Daniel 6: There and Back Again – A Deity's Tale.*" HTS Teologiese Studies/Theological Studies. 6.

23 Walton, Matthews, and Chavalas. *The IVP Bible Background Commentary.* InterVarsity Press, 2000. 739.

ed, reminds us of Christ's experience of having those who hated his faithfulness to God plot against him to have him killed and placed into a tomb with a rock covering it, only to emerge unharmed proclaiming God's salvation and power.

By saving Daniel from death amid the lions, Daniel's God showed everyone multiple things that day. Daniel's God was not only present in Jerusalem. He was present in Babylon, in the lion's den, and He was present and in opposition to the decree of the king. Daniel's God transcended land and legal codes. Daniel 6 ended with the king celebrating Daniel's salvation and ordering Daniel's false accusers and their families to experience the same fate they had devised for Daniel. They were thrown into the lion's den. The difference was that their gods could not save them from the jaws of the lions, and they were all devoured.

Although God's saving act is at the forefront of Daniel 6, I do not believe that is the primary purpose of the passage. I believe the big picture of Daniel 6 is that God's power transcends location and law. Dr. Joyce Baldwin says,

> Persecution is not the point (of the stories shared in Daniel)…The episodes chosen demonstrate that the world's great empires, and the kings who represent them, are all subject to the God of the exiles from Judah, who made Himself known outside the land of promise as well as within it.[24]

Yes, Daniel 6 does explore the conflict Daniel experienced as he sought to remain faithful to his God amid the political jockeying of his fellow leaders. But I think that is part of the backdrop to the larger truth that God wants us to understand. That larger truth is that God is not bound by location or legal wrangling that some believe place them in positions above God and God's people. God will always show God's strength, no matter where people try to place God or God's people. Dr. Joseph de Bruyn expresses this truth much better than I can when he says, "Daniel 6 is not just a story about the character Daniel being persecuted for his faith;

---

24 Baldwin. *Daniel.* InterVarsity Press, 1978. 119.

rather it is a story about the God of Israel establishing his presence and his ability to act through and within space and time." God's presence and ability to act are greater than any location or man-made obstacle.

A secondary truth I think we can hang our hats on is found in the parallels between Daniel's lion's den experience and those of our Savior, Jesus. No human plan or law is too wise, and no pit is too deep or filled with enough lions, to keep God from responding on our behalf. As we regularly find ourselves considering the implications of the life, death, and resurrection of our Savior, may we remember this truth and trust that God is not bound by location or law. He can and does respond whenever and wherever His children call on His name.

CONCLUSION

What does an ancient document like the Book of Daniel have to do with anything going on in the 21st Century? At the time of this writing, the all-consuming challenge we all face is COVID-19 and its aftereffects. Although there are specific calculations for the numbers of people infected, the lives lost, and the economic and cultural impact of this worldwide pandemic, the physical, psychological, and economic suffering that has occurred is truly unmeasurable.

One of the unspoken challenges of this current pandemic and the efforts to combat it is that COVID-19 will eventually pass, but there will likely be another national or global challenge that will emerge, or reemerge, quickly to replace it. Suffering and misfortune will not end. Instead, they will take another form. Another disease or virus will eventually ravage our communities. Another dictator will rise to power. Another shockwave will occur that causes unforeseen ripples to travel through the world.

The Book of Daniel reminds us that no matter the hardship experienced by people or what occurs in the world, God is still aware and has plans to bring about good in the life of God's creation. God may seem to be silent, but God is not. God is still actively involved today, as was true in Daniel. No other god, world catastrophe, or personal disaster is greater than the One whom we have placed our trust in. This acknowledgment and understanding of God's power does not always guarantee that life will be easier or that we will not experience times of significant pain. What it can do is give us hope and peace as we navigate unfamiliar territory and await a sign from heaven that reminds us that our pain and suffering will soon be over, and joy and peace are on the way. Amen.

Sources

Baldwin, Joyce. *Daniel.* InterVarsity Press, 1978.

Carson, Donald A., R. T. France, J. A. Motyer, and G. J. Wenham (editors). *New Bible Commentary: 21st Century Edition.* InterVarsity Press, 1994.

De Bruyn, Joseph J., 2015, 'Daniel 6: There and back again – A deity's tale', HTS Teologiese Studies/Theological Studies 71(3), Art. #2110, 8 pages. http://dx.doi.org/10.4102/ hts. v71i3.2110.

Keck, Leander E. (editor). *The New Interpreter's Bible Volume VII: Introduction to Apocalyptic Literature, Daniel, and the Minor Prophets.* Abingdon Press, 1997.

Lewis, Clive Staples. *The Problem of Pain.* Harper One, 1996.

Pace, Sharon. *Daniel.* Smyth & Helwys, 2008.

Towner, Wayne Sibley. *Daniel.* John Knox Press, 2012.

Walton, John H., Victor H. Matthews, and Mark W. Chavalas. *The IVP Bible Background Commentary.* InterVarsity Press, 2000.

Walvoord, John F., and Robert B. Zuck (editors). *The Bible Knowledge Commentary: An Exposition of the Scriptures.* Victor Books, 1985.

Widder, Wendy. *Daniel.* Zondervan, 2016.

Black and Brown Christians in America often live in a world that is separated from that of White Christians, with White Christians seemingly unaware of their concerns. Can these groups function as effective parts of the Body of Christ?

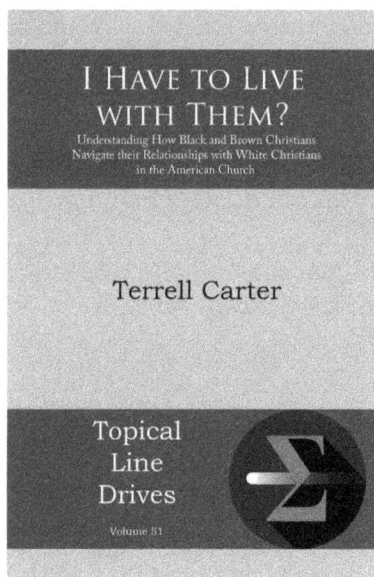

I HAVE TO LIVE WITH THEM?

Understanding How Black and Brown Christians Navigate their Relationships with White Christians in the American Church

Terrell Carter

Topical Line Drives

Volume 51

In *I Have to Live with Them?* Dr. Terrell Carter works to bridge the gap in our understanding and thus help to find the way for us to work together. Is the church functioning as a positive force in society? Shouldn't we be talking more about the gospel and less about race? What can we do when we find that, rather than a solution, we ourselves are part of the problem? Is there accountability for the damage done historically?

In this very short treatment, you'll find some answers to these questions and some pointers toward ways of facing these issues squarely and finding positive ways forward.

https://www.energiondirect.com/product/i-have-to-live-with-them

www.ingramcontent.com/pod-product-compliance
Lightning Source LLC
LaVergne TN
LVHW041207080426
835508LV00008B/835